SHAD HELMSTETTER, PH.D.

Best-Selling Author of
What to Say When You Talk to Your Self

A
60-Minute
Book

SELF-TALK
for
STRESS

ANXIETY
&
DEPRESSION

Self-Talk for
Stress
Anxiety
and
Depression

By Shad Helmstetter, Ph.D.

Self-Talk for Stress, Anxiety and Depression

Published by Park Avenue Press
362 Gulf Breeze Pkwy., #104
Gulf Breeze, FL 32561
©2020 by Shad Helmstetter. All rights reserved.

Helmstetter, Shad
Self-Talk for Stress, Anxiety and Depression

ISBN: 978-1-7344982-3-3

Table of Contents

Chapter One

A Message of Sunlight

"The answer to almost all stress lies in our self-talk. It isn't the problem itself; it's the way we perceive the problem that causes the stress."
— *Shad Helmstetter*

All of us feel stressed or anxious or even depressed—at least from time to time. But what

1

if we feel those pressures too often, or they become too great to bear?

What can you do when life is difficult and it seems like there is nothing you can do to make it better? Where can you turn when stress and anxiety hang like shrouds of despair in the recesses of your mind, darkening your days, and turning them into unending night?

We live at a time when things are changing, when times are difficult and unsure. Today, things feel uncertain, and insecurity is a way of life. It's that way for all of us. No one escapes it.

So why is it, then, that while most of the world struggles with unknowns and fear and stress and anxiety, some people move through it almost as though they are protected from the troubles that surround them?

Why are some people able to deal with the same problems everyone else has without feeling the same stresses? What makes them different, safer, somehow? Do they know a secret the rest of the world doesn't know?

In fact there *is* a secret. It's a secret that can help keep at least some of the stress and the fear at bay. It is a truth some people have discovered that allows them to walk through the darkness—and not only survive, but thrive! This book is about that secret—the secret that lets the sunlight in.

* * *

Over the last forty years, I have researched the subject of self-talk, and what self-talk can do to help us improve our lives. During that time, I've written more than twenty books on the subject. Those books have dealt with self-talk and personal programming, especially as it relates to helping us live better lives—living out the promise and potential we were born with.

The book you're reading now focuses on a very specific and important problem—an unhealthy amount of stress and anxiety, and the depression that often accompanies them. In this book, you'll find specific steps you can take to reduce the role these unwelcome challenges play in your life.

Because you're reading this book, I can assume you may have already explored dealing with stress and its accompanying problems in a variety of ways. Those could include counseling or therapy, pharmaceutical interventions, physical exercise, or meditation, among others.

I do not suggest that the self-talk techniques we'll be discussing here should replace any of these remedies that may work for you. The information and techniques we discuss here should prove to augment those remedies and help them work even more effectively in relieving the stress, anxiety, or depression you're experiencing.

There are various causes and conditions that lead to anxiety or depression. Some of these are based on common imbalances in brain chemistry, and others are created by external circumstances that lead to stress-inducing mental states.

But most of the causes are directly affected by the way we think about challenges and how we deal with them—which is directly influenced by our self-talk and the messages we wire into our brain.

Depression itself has many forms and causes. We're not talking here only about the kind of depression that results from physical/chemical issues; here we're focusing on the kind of depression that comes from living with unrelenting stress and anxiety—day after day, for so long that your world turns gray and stays that way.

It's a dark, vicious cycle that works like this: A negative mindset makes depression worse. The worsened depression creates an even more negative mindset. That creates more depression . . . which once again makes the negative mindset worse. It's a cycle that can be unending, but it's a cycle that can also be broken.

Covering the Basics

In these pages, we'll cover the basics of self-talk—what it is and how it works, the important science behind it, and how to apply what we have learned about self-talk to the problem of stress and anxiety in your life.

If you're reading the printed edition of this book, you'll notice that it is printed in larger type, in an open format, with fewer pages than a standard, full-length book. That's because this book is written in a more accessible '60-Minute Book' format. This format is designed to give you as much information as possible in the shortest possible time (about an hour of reading).

It is my hope that what you find in these pages will give you the information you need to help you create more peace of mind and well-being in your life—today and every day to come.

Chapter Two

A Brief History of Self-Talk

If you're not familiar with the kind of self-talk we're discussing in this book, you could think that 'self-talk' refers to the picture of someone walking down the street mumbling or talking out loud to themselves, with other people thinking they're crazy for doing it.

But the kind of self-talk this book is about is very different from that. This book is about the messages we give to our own brains day after day, and how the messages our brain receives wire us to deal with life in specific ways—good and bad. And that includes both how stress is created in our lives, and how we deal with it.

The idea of self-talk is very old—it is referenced in the Bible—but the science that led to the understanding of self-talk has only been with us for the past few decades. My own interest in self-talk was born after I had served as a foreign language interpreter for the United States government in Cuba during the Cuban Missile Crisis.

I was deeply interested in understanding how the human brain becomes programmed, and how our mental programs become imbedded in our brains. Because I had studied foreign languages, I recognized that mental programming was very much like learning a language—imprinting a vocabulary that both controls and expresses our thoughts, and ultimately structures our beliefs.

It was clear to me that our self-talk, the 'language' we think in—the actual vocabulary we use throughout each day—plays a significant role in determining not only how we think, but also how we see the world each day. The question I asked was, *"What if we could change how we see the world, and how we deal with life, by changing the language we use when we talk to ourselves?"*

The idea made sense. But as I began what would become decades of study and research into how to reprogram the human brain for success in life, I had no idea how accurate that first assumption was: *we become most what we think most.*

In the early 1980s, even before I began to write books on the subject, my first public step into the world of self-talk was to write and produce an extensive series of recorded self-talk audio sessions that would teach the listener a new internal language—a positive new vocabulary—exactly like learning a new foreign language.

This time, however, the new language would be a language that would focus on 'life success.' The recorded self-talk sessions were based on the proven concepts of personal responsibility, self-belief, setting goals, and taking positive action, and they helped the listeners imprint clear, new thought patterns in their brains.

The concept worked extremely well, and the result was that, suddenly, there were people from all walks of life who were starting their day each morning by listening to recorded self-talk sessions. The subjects they listened to included things like weight loss, relationships, career improvement, and financial success. By listening to these early self-talk sessions every day, people were literally rewiring their brains with completely new mental programs—a new language of success.

What the early self-talk listeners proved was that, with a minimum amount of effort, any individual could actually *change* what they thought, and how they thought—and therefore the action they would take—as a result of the new 'language' they were learning.

I had started this research by using myself as my first test subject. At the time, I needed to lose weight, but I had failed miserably at every diet I had tried. Because of my interest in self-talk, I came to the conclusion that my weight problem might actually be a problem of overweight *thinking*—how I thought about weight, diet, and exercise, and everything that went along with it.

So I decided to change my self-talk. By listening each day to recordings of very healthy self-talk, in the next 10 ½ weeks, I lost 58 pounds! I was convinced. But what really proved the point was that, this time, the weight didn't come back! (Now, forty years later, it still hasn't.)

As I continued to study the concept of self-talk and what it could do, I began to recognize that not only were the results real, but that the concept could work with anyone. I saw, even then, the potential impact that changing a person's self-talk could have in their lives, and I was very concerned that the idea of permanently changing one's self-talk should not be tossed into the bin with 'wishful thinking' or short-term motivation.

I knew that, applied correctly, self-talk was *foundational*. It was a deeper, and profoundly important, insight into how the human brain becomes programmed for success or for failure in anything.

To that end, in 1985, I founded the Self-Talk Institute. It remains, to this day, the world's leading organization in the field of self-talk. It is the objective of the Institute to study the science and application of self-talk techniques, and to make learning self-talk available to individuals worldwide.

To reach that goal, the Institute has trained and certified several hundred self-talk trainers who teach the message of self-talk to audiences throughout the United States and in other countries. The Institute also maintains a very popular website (www.selftalkplus.com), which streams recorded self-talk learning sessions every day to listeners around the world.

The concept of self-talk has also become a major factor in how human behavior is understood in the academic world. Self-talk, and the wiring of the human brain, is at the core of recent advancements in the fields of psychology, sports, health, and education, among others. Self-talk—both the positive and the negative kind—is now recognized as playing a role in every facet of human development and expression.

Your own self-talk today is playing a pivotal, directing role in every important area of your life. Your health, your relationships, your career, your income, your well-being, and not surprisingly, your *stress*, are all directed or influenced by your self-talk.

What we have learned specifically about self-talk and stress is encouraging and uplifting. If you suffer any of the pain and despair that stress and anxiety bring to our lives, I want to assure you there is more than hope. There is something you can do about it. Understanding what self-talk is and how to use it to reduce your stress and anxiety can make a difference. It is a tool that is changing lives, for the better, every day.

Chapter Three

Where Your Programs Begin

From the moment you were born, every message you received was recorded in your brain. Everything you hear, everything you see, everything you think, everything you say, everything you experience, is recorded in your brain—temporarily.

Then, every message you receive that is *repeated* often enough is wired into your brain 'permanently' as a new program in your brain's computer-like operating system. The result is that the programs you have received—about anything—have been wired into your brain, and those programs determine what you believe—about anything.

It doesn't make any difference if the programs you received were 'true' or not. The part of the brain that stores those programs doesn't know the difference between something that's true and something that's false.

Your brain just stores the programs it gets— and it acts on those programs as though they are *true*. (This is why so many people can be so wrong about so many things, and still believe they're right—their brains are *wired* to believe they're right.)

The 148,000 *No's*

It has been estimated that the average person, growing up in a reasonably positive home, is told *'no,'* or what they *'cannot'* do,

17

more than 148,000 times during the first 18 years of their life alone!

In your own life, during that time, how many times were you told how *exceptional* you were, what you *could* do, or what you *could* become?

Even if you were fortunate, with parents or role models who showed you your true potential, it is likely that the thousands of *no's* you received from the rest of the world were not balanced out by the *yes's* you received during the same time.

The result of that kind of programming is that we end up where we are today, with our brains improperly wired, or often wired to work *against* us.

The Newborn Nursery

Most of us have had the opportunity to visit a hospital's newborn nursery, where we first look in on precious little infants just after they're born. In the nursery, we usually observe the infants through a viewing window. There, on the other side of the window, snuggled in their little bassinets, we see those remarkable miracles of life.

Imagine looking in on a couple of those infants right now. They are amazing! If they're awake, and their eyes are open, we can see them looking out at their world for the first time, as though they're searching for that incredible life they were born to live.

When we look into the eyes of those infants, what we see is *unlimited opportunity and endless possibility*. They have their entire lives in front of them. Their potential is infinite. And it's clear that each of those infants was born to succeed! (*No one* is born to fail.) In fact, everything about those little infants is designed to help each of them reach their greatest potential and live a life that fulfills their highest promise. That's what they were born to do!

But, then, even as they leave the warm, comfortable security of their birthing bassinet and a short stay in a hospital room, the first moments of the infant's programming begins. From the mother's first words, to the television screen in the corner of the room, messages begin to feed into that child's brain.

Mothers and fathers, brothers, sisters, other family members, and, in time, friends, teachers, media, the internet, and every other programming source in that young person's life join in with message after message—and the child's brain is designed to take it all in.

As the child continues to grow, whatever they hear often enough is forming, in their brain, the picture of who that child believes himself or herself to be, and what is 'true' about anything. Almost everything they think is being formed by the repetition of programs they receive.

It doesn't make any difference if the programs they receive are actually true or not.

With enough repetition, *any* program can become *truth* in the child's brain.

To illustrate this, imagine that instead of being born, brought home, and raised as you were, in the home you were raised in, you had been kidnapped as an infant and taken to a different home, brought up in a completely different country, and raised by different parents in a different part of the world.

Instead of being 'you,' with the name and the family and the friends and the education and the experience and the beliefs you have now, you would be the product of an entirely different environment. You would still be 'you' genetically, but everything else about 'you' would be different. Your beliefs about almost everything—your faith, your ideology, your habits, the way you dress, your attitudes, your work, your relationships, your goals, and your future would have changed. Virtually everything about you would be different.

In fact, if that had actually happened, you could even view the person you are in your real life today as an *enemy*—and you could think and believe the *opposite* of almost everything you think and believe today.

We are all born to excel—to live up to our greatest promise, with our whole lives in front of us. But then, all too often, something happens that interrupts that process—and it can change everything. Not as dramatic as being stolen from our crib, perhaps, but something happens to us that *does* redirect, and often changes, the course of the rest of our life.

The programs we receive end up forming what we believe, and what we think about everything. Our programs tell us who we are, and even what we will—or will *not* do—every day of our lives.

Where 'Success' and 'Failure' Begin

Take a moment, right now, while you're reading this, and think of someone you know, or know of, whom you would consider to be a truly 'successful' person.

I don't mean just financially successful, but successful in *life*. This would be someone whose life is working! Someone who is living a life that is fulfilled, and always moving upwards. It would probably be someone you would like to get to know, or spend time with and learn from.

Your picture could be of someone who is living now or someone who isn't. But whoever it is, get a clear picture of that 'most successful' person in your mind now.

Now, while you're holding a picture of that person in your mind, I'd like you to imagine that she or he is actually there with you. In your mind's eye, imagine that that person is standing not too far from you, off to the right of you. And for the moment, we'll just ask that person to stand there.

Then, with the successful person waiting calmly and patiently, we're going to add someone else to our experiment.

To do this, I would like you now to think of someone you would see as the *least* successful person you know. This could be someone you know, or know of, but someone who is literally 'failing' at life.

When I think of the least successful person I know, I see the picture of a young kid who left home because of drug use when he was seventeen years old, and his parents have never seen him since. If they did find him, now, years later, they would probably find him in an alley somewhere, and he probably wouldn't even recognize his own parents because of the amount of drugs or chemicals in his system.

That's the person who comes to my mind when I think of someone who is 'failing' in every way. But in your own mind, think of an example of someone you know, or know of, who fits your picture of failure. Whoever it is, get a clear image of that person in your mind.

Then, imagine that person is also there with you right now, and is standing off to the left of you.

Now, in this experiment, you should have two people standing near you. Off to your right is the person who is *succeeding* in life. On your left is the person who is *failing* in life.

Take a moment and examine each of them. Get a good picture of them in your mind.

One of them—the successful one on the right—is living a life that works. Successful in every important way. Uplifting and fulfilling. Happy, and feeling good about life.

The other person—the unsuccessful one on the left—is failing and spiraling downward. Unhappy, and living a life that is not working.

The Answer

This next question holds one of the most important answers you can ever know:

What is the real difference between the two people? What is the difference between the person whose life is working and the person whose life is not working?

The answer is: The difference between the two people is their *programs*.

It is their programs, given to them after they were born, that caused them to live their lives in different ways—and created the success or failure each of them has now.

To prove how true this is, all you have to do is to imagine that those two people *could have been the two infants we saw in the newborn nursery just a short time ago*—with their eyes wide open, searching, each of them waiting to live out the unlimited potential they were born to achieve.

And now, after time has passed, and their brains were wired, and the programs took hold, here they are, *completely different* from each other in the outcome of their lives.

That difference reveals one of the most important truths we can ever learn about human behavior, and even about life itself.

When they were born, the opportunity to grow into a complete and fulfilled person was the same for each of them. But one of them ended up being wired to succeed. The other one ended up being wired to fail.

People who argue against this would tell you that it was just life's challenges, its ups and downs, that got in the way and changed the infant who failed. And they would say that it was good luck or fortune that interceded and made the successful person successful. Or they might say that it was just the difference in the two individuals' DNA.

But that's not the answer. The person who receives better, healthier, more positive programs will, over time, virtually always do better than the person who receives unhealthy, negative programs.

If you know someone who is doing really well, year after year, and continues to do so in spite of life's challenges—that's *programs*. If you know someone who is failing, time after time, and continues to fail, and even with help can't seem to get life right—that's programs.

What Are Your Programs Now?

As you probably guessed from the above picture, it's clear that when you're dealing with stress and anxiety, you should start by looking at your programs—and begin to recognize the programs that are creating the stress and anxiety in the first place.

If any of your self-talk is inaccurate, or self-defeating—which creates bad programs—

change it. Choose to wire your own brain with the right, positive programs—the ones that should have been given to you in the first place. And, forever, get rid of the self-talk that works against you. Get rid of the self-talk that's negative.

Chapter Four

Negative Self-Talk

Most of us can understand that when we were growing up, we got programmed. And we end up living out the programs we got—whether they were good programs or bad.

Our Negative Self-Talk

It is because of our programming that we have so much negative self-talk. That's why we hear ourselves saying things like:

"I can't handle this."

"Nothing ever goes right for me."

"I'm just frazzled today."

"The stress is killing me."

"I'm really on edge."

"I worry all the time."

"I can't seem to relax."

"That's impossible!"

"Why even try?"

"When will I ever learn?"

"There's just no way."

"I don't know what to do."

"I'm a nervous wreck."

"I just know it won't work out."

"My life is a mess."

"If something could go wrong, it will!"

"That really makes me mad."

"I get sick just thinking about it."

"I get so depressed."

"I wish I could be happy."

"What if I lose my job?"

"What if I get sick?"

"I just can't take it any more."

"I'm really at the end of my rope."

"There's nothing I can do."

"I'm at my wits' end!"

"Today just isn't my day."

Every one of those simple messages is negative. Every one of them is harmful. And every one of them is a *directive* to your brain.

Can you imagine typing directions like those into your mental computer? Especially if your brain is going to accept them as *truth?* We do it all the time. And the more you say them or think them, the more *wired-in* and *true* those directions become!

Negative self-talk goes far beyond those few, simple examples, of course. It enters into and influences virtually every area of our lives.

Here are a few more examples. Have you ever said anything like any of the following? Read through the list carefully and see if you find yourself in any of them:

"The only luck I have is bad luck."

"I'm so clumsy!"

"I'm so stupid."

"What a loser!"

"I'm too shy."

"I never know what to say."

"I never win anything."

"I just wasn't cut out for that."

"I don't have the energy I used to."

"Nobody likes me."

"I never make enough money."

"Everything I touch turns to bleep."

"I can never get ahead."

"Nobody listens to me."

"I never know what to do."

"I'm not smart enough."

"I'm no good at math."

"I'm just not creative."

"I just wasn't cut out for that."

"I can never lose weight."

"Everything I eat goes right to my waist."

"I take weight off and it comes right back on again."

"My kids are driving me crazy."

"This will be the death of me yet."

"I can never seem to get organized."

"I already know I won't like it."

"I never have enough time."

"I don't have the patience for that."

"I never have enough money left over at the end of the month."

"When will I ever learn?"

"That's just my luck."

"Why even try?"

"It's just no use."

Those examples represent just a hint of the language that directs countless lives toward stress and failure, instead of peace and well-being. When you even *think* them, or thousands of other negative self-talk messages just like them, even when they pass unnoticed through your mind, *you are wiring your brain to make them true. You are wiring your brain to fail.*

And those examples are just a few of the *simple*, obvious kinds of self-talk we use against ourselves. A lot of negative self-talk is much more complex than that, the kind that allows us to see an entire picture of our lives as failing, and never living up to how we wish things could have been.

This is especially true of the negative self-talk that creates stress, or deals with stress badly—the kind of dark, depressing self-talk that is woven throughout our thoughts each day, and creates an entire attitude of hopelessness. It programs the brain to operate in a way that makes it impossible to get rid of the stress that's crippling you.

Negative self-talk does that because of the way *the brain is designed to work*. Fortunately, as we will see, understanding what's happening in your brain will help you fix the problem.

Chapter Five

Self-Talk and Your Brain

The process by which self-talk rewires your brain is somewhat complicated. Here is a simplified overview of how it works.

The Neuroplasticity of Your Brain

Neuroplasticity refers to your brain's ability to form new neural networks and connections based on new input. This process takes place throughout your lifetime.

This means that your brain is always learning, and it is always changing. New learning or experience actually changes the physical structure—the wiring—of your brain.

Research into the brain's neuroplasticity has opened new doors of treatment for stroke victims, as well as for people who struggle with dyslexia, learning disorders, and even brain damage.

The key here is that research in the field of neuroscience has identified the link between your thoughts and how your brain is wired. What you experience, what you think, and what you say changes the synaptic connections in your brain.

And that means that what you have been thinking and saying—without being aware of it—has been wiring and changing your brain.

Your Brain Believes What It is Told Most

Deep inside the workings of the human brain, there is no actual *'truth.'* The part of the brain that stores all of the messages you have received accepts what it is told most often—and these become the strongest messages. The brain then plays those messages back to you, and as I noted earlier, it presents them to you as 'truth' or 'fact,' whether the messages are actually true or not.

That's why you can believe in one political ideology completely, when the other half of the population—many millions of people—believes in the opposite political ideology. And you, and all of them, think that your own beliefs are correct. (A perfect example of this is that many people, when voting, are actually voting based on the programmed biases that have been wired, through repetition, into their brains—not on the actual qualifications of the candidate.)

This is also why you can consistently stress about something that very probably will not harm you; it is because your brain is ultimately trying to protect you. (More on this later.) It is wired to focus on the worst first, and the best last.

It is that focus, born of fear, that is the home of almost all of the stress we experience in our life. All stress is created by fear—and most fears are false.

Unless you change them, *most* of the programs your brain is focusing on are the wrong programs. They're not true at all—but your brain and your stress don't know that.

Are Your Programs Helping You or Hurting You?

What you believe about anything is not a measure of its correctness. What you believe about anything is a measure of the programs you have that support your belief.

Just as with your political beliefs, your brain has stored an immense number of programs about *you*—everything you believe to be true about you.

If enough of your programs are negative, your self-talk will also be negative. This is because your present self-talk is the result of the programs you already have that are the strongest. The rule is: Negative programs equal negative self-talk.

And it is in negative and inaccurate programs, that most of your stress and anxiety live.

Neuroplasticity and Repetition

You'll notice that, in these pages, I have occasionally repeated certain points of information that are especially important. There is a reason for the repetition. Reading something more than once, or several times, helps to ensure that the brain will wire the information into its long-term memory. Repetition increases retention.

It is also repetition that plays the greatest role in wiring your brain to create stress—or to lessen it. Because of the brain's neuroplasticity, the most important key to wiring or rewiring your brain is repetition. The brain is designed to pay attention to, and store, the messages that are repeated most often.

Here's how it works: A message your brain receives only once will be stored in your brain's short-term memory only briefly. It doesn't become 'wired in' to your brain's long-term storage files. But when that same message is repeated frequently, your brain begins to form new neural connections. It wires the new message into, and connects it with, the vast neural networks of your conscious and unconscious mind.

And it is because your brain stores messages that are repeated that *you end up believing the things about you that you tell yourself most.* The complete 'you' that you believe you are today is the combined result of years of messages you have received from the world around you, and—most importantly—the repeated messages you have been giving yourself through your own self-talk.

This means that whatever messages you got from others, combined with what your experiences have caused you to say to yourself in your own self-talk, have created everything you believe to be true about yourself today.

Some of the messages your brain received about you may have been true. But many of the messages your brain received and wired in were not true at all!

Together, those inaccurate messages, through lifelong repetition, have created every negative belief you have about yourself today. Your self-doubts, your imagined inadequacies, most of your fears, and everything you believe incorrectly about who you are today, are the result of the repetition of inaccurate messages to your brain.

If the programming of the brain is based on repetition, and if your own self-talk is negative, and tells you that you cannot solve the problem or overcome the challenge in front of you, what is the only outcome you can predict?

The only outcome you can predict is uncertainty, fear, anxiety, and *stress*.

As we've learned, we continually—and unconsciously—repeat and replay the programs we get most often. (In the brain, the strongest program always wins.) And this gives us an insight into where our stress comes from: *Most of our stress is the result of mental programs that tell us what we cannot overcome.*

The solution to most of our harmful stress is clear—we need to rewire our brains with something more 'positive.' But isn't positive thinking nothing more than 'wishful' thinking? Let's take a look.

Your Prefrontal Cortex

At one time, skeptics did believe that "positive thinking" was nothing more than wishful thinking, and that the idea of positive thinking was something you could read about in a self-help book, but it wouldn't really make your life any better. Subsequent brain research, however, has shown an entirely different story.

People who have trained their brains to think in the *positive,* actually wire more neural networks into the *left* prefrontal cortex of their brain. (Reach up and tap the area just above your *left* eyebrow.) That's a part of the brain that helps you seek options and alternatives, *helps you find a better way to deal with problems,* boosts your attitude, and puts you into positive action.

Obviously, having good, strong wiring in that part of your brain is *essential.* And positive self-talk *strengthens* that part of your brain! The remarkable summary is: *Positive thinking strengthens the part of the brain that helps you succeed.*

And what about negative self-talkers? People who habitually think in the *negative* wire more neural networks into the *right* prefrontal cortex of their brains. (Now tap just above your *right* eyebrow.) That's a part of the brain that causes you to *shut down your options,* makes you feel down or depressed, puts you into escape mode, and stops you from solving the problem or taking the action you should be taking.

In short, *negative thinking strengthens the part of the brain that helps you fail.*

(If you tapped your forehead just now, did you automatically think of yourself as having a stronger *left* prefrontal cortex, or a stronger *right* prefrontal cortex? That is, do you see yourself as more of a positive thinker, or as someone who has more negative thoughts?)

Today, breakthroughs in neuroscience that tell us why self-talk is a major player in our behavior—and our individual well-being in life—have become commonplace. Neuroscience has identified the essential importance of positive attitudes and even where they reside in the brain. And the takeaway from our current understanding of brain physiology makes it clear that our thoughts not only become wired into our brain—they change the *structure* of the brain itself.

Self-Talk and Your Subconscious Mind

Your subconscious mind makes most of your choices for you—without your being aware of it.

That's kind of scary, when you recognize that as much as 90% or more of your mental programs are buried in your subconscious mind—*and are completely hidden from you!* It is safe to say that you have virtually tens of thousands of programs that are directing your life right now, and you are not actually aware of what most of those programs are.

It has been estimated that, in the average individual, 77% or more of their unconscious programs are *negative* and may be working against them. This means that not only is your subconscious mind silently making most of your choices for you, but it is also making those choices based on programs that are mostly negative.

The obvious solution to this problem is to find a practical way to wire enough positive *new* programs into your brain, so that your subconscious mind is controlled by positive programs—not negative ones.

But before we look at the best ways to do that—and begin to lower your stress and anxiety for good—there is one more stress-maker we have to contend with. And it's the granddaddy of all stress-makers.

Chapter Six

Your Hidden Alarm

Before we can solve the problem of stress and anxiety, we have to look at one final actor– –and the critical role it plays in setting you up for stress. It's your hidden alarm system; it's called the *amygdala*.

The amygdala is a small, partially almond-shaped structure—located in the approximate center of the brain—that plays a key role in managing *emotion* and *fear*. In the simplest terms, one of the jobs of the amygdala is to alert you to any danger that may be lurking nearby.

It was designed to keep people safe from saber-toothed tigers, or anything else that could hurt them when they still lived in the wild, untamed jungles of the past.

The problem is, we don't live in wild, untamed jungles anymore, and there are no longer any saber-toothed tigers lurking in the shadows, ready to attack us. But the amygdala doesn't know the saber-tooth tigers are gone, and it doesn't know we don't need the same hyper-sensitive alarm system to keep us alive these days. So, the amygdala continues to alert us to any and every possible sign of danger—just like it was designed to do in the distant past.

Unfortunately, the amygdala doesn't know the difference between a danger that is *real*, and one that is *imagined*; the alarm it triggers and stress it creates are exactly the same! This means that much of the stress you feel each day is being triggered by an alarm system that is constantly sending you *false* alarms.

Getting a phone call in the middle of the night is a good example. A split second after the first sound of the phone ringing hits your ears, the amygdala responds! Your internal silent alarm goes off, and your brain goes into high alert, even before you're awake enough to know what's happening. *"Danger, danger, Will Robinson!"* your brain is shouting. Meanwhile, the stress hormones dopamine, cortisol, epinephrine, and norepinephrine are being pumped into your system, instantly giving you a mental and physical kick that's almost painful. *The phone is ringing! Someone's in trouble! Something's wrong!*

That same scenario plays out even if it's a wrong number, of course. It didn't make a single bit of difference to your amygdala that nothing was actually *wrong*. It turned all of your alert senses on high *just in case* something *might* be wrong.

The setup to your next bout of stress could be an unexpected letter in your mailbox, a rumor that your company may be downsizing, the ATM not taking your card, a call from your son or daughter's school, or your doctor saying he needs to talk to you—almost anything at all will alert the amygdala to sound the alarm.

And, unfortunately, most people don't have to get bad news from someone else for their alarm system to get set off. They do it in their head! All you have to do is think of something you're worried about for even a moment, and bam!, your alarm goes off. Your amygdala thinks you're in trouble, and instantly dumps more stress chemicals into your system, and . . . here we go again!

In addition to getting set off for no good reason, the amygdala also wields a double-edged sword that makes things even worse: Stress increases the action of the amygdala, and the action of the amygdala increases the stress response. So it becomes a vicious cycle—an out-of-control amygdala creates more stress, and an increase in your stress tells your amygdala to stay on high alert. Untamed, it is not a win-win situation; it's a lose-lose.

Imagine, then, what happens when your over-active amygdala teams up with your overly-negative self-talk. When it does, all bets are off. Suddenly, it's mental chaos! The alarm bells are clanging and your self-talk goes into total negative and makes everything triple-worse. You are no longer in control. Even good things look bad. Promise and hope fly out the window. The only thing left in the room is tension and panic—and your stress level goes through the roof!

Even the left-over residue of that kind of stress can create anxiety that lasts for days.

Too many people have too much of that in their lives. Their days are filled with mental trauma, endless anxiety fills their hours, their own overly-activated brain and their self-defeating self-talk conspire against them—with no foreseeable end in sight. Tomorrow will be just like today, more stress, more worry, and no help on the way. (It's no wonder so many people dangerously self-medicate; they're trying to quiet their self-talk and turn off their amygdala!)

Now imagine the *opposite* of that stress cycle happening. Imagine turning down your alarm system with the kind of self-talk that calms it and quiets it, replacing your worries and fears with solutions, strengths, and positive possibilities. In doing that, you're not relying on blind hope; you're calling up practical answers you have within you. You're telling your brain to help you see what you *can* do, instead of what you *cannot.*

Calming your amygdala—managing your fears—doesn't mean you should hide from problems or try to block things you need to address. It's the *unnecessary* alerts we're talking about here, the worry and the fear that are created or exaggerated in your mind, even if they're not an actual threat in real life.

With the right self-talk, you can send a message to the amygdala that has been triggering the stress hormones you've been inadvertently pouring into your system. With the right self-talk, you can play an active role in regulating it.

In time, you may even come to a whole new set of terms with yourself: what makes you afraid; what triggers your stress and anxiety; how you reframe stress and anxiety in your own mind, and how you diminish their strength and their power in your life.

There is no magic in this; the brain is designed to do what you tell it most. Changing your language to the right kind of self-talk can become one of your greatest allies in helping you turn off the unnecessary alarms—and the unnecessary stress they've been creating in your life.

Chapter Seven

Positive Self-Talk

So much of our stress comes from a poorly-wired picture of life! Harmful self-talk destroys our spirits, fills us with anxiety, causes us to doubt and fear, and, all too often, fail.

What if it is the unnoticed, unhealthy, self-defeating words of negative self-talk that are causing the stress you're feeling? What if your own self-talk has been wiring your brain with a false, dark picture of life, and you're living in that darkness every day?

And what if you decided to change that? What could happen then?

We have learned that when people change their self-talk, they get rid of unnecessary negatives—and the stress that goes along with them. This would tell you that if you want to reduce your stress, changing your self-talk is not only a good idea—it is essential!

To become familiar with the kind of self-talk that has proven to help, here are examples of positive self-talk that show you a less stressful picture of you. As you read these examples, take your time, read them carefully, let them sink in, and imagine them describing you as you really are:

"I choose to think in a healthy way. I have learned to choose the thoughts that create calm within me, and give me peace of mind."

"I never let unnecessary stress or anxiety play any role in my life."

"I choose to be relaxed, and free of tension and worry of any kind."

"When I feel stress, and want to let it go, I take three, slow, deep breaths; feel deeply thankful I am here—and let myself know that for me, all is well with the world."

"I choose to see the world in a bright, positive, promising way. That's what I choose, that's what I see, and that's what I create."

"Creating peace of mind comes easily and naturally to me now. I choose it, I create it, and I live it."

"I am calm and confident, and I feel a deep sense of peace within me."

"I make sure I take the time to rest, relax, and create balance in my life."

"I consciously remove all unnecessary stress from my life. I am happy to be here, and *thankful for the opportunity to grow, and live up to my best."*

"I have inner peace. I am living my life in a positive and worthwhile way. "

"I have purpose and value. I like who I am, and I enjoy being me. This creates even greater peace and self-assurance within me."

"Each day I recognize and appreciate the many blessings in my life."

"The more I am aware of my blessings, the more of them I find."

"I am never afraid to face challenges or deal with problems."

"I confront conflicts, I deal with them, and I resolve them. "

"I never over-commit. I am in control of my time, my life, and every breath I take."

"I'm good at getting things done, on time, and in the right way."

"I do everything I need to do, when I need to do it. "

"Right now, I let go of any tension I might have. And I can feel myself becoming calm and relaxed."

"I never allow harmful tension to build up inside of me. I conquer stress by conquering its causes."

"I never let stress become more important than it should be in my life."

"I choose to be calm and relaxed. I know that I have the ability to overcome any problem I am facing."

"Every day, I consciously create calm and peace in my life."

"The more I see myself as calm and in control, the more peace of mind I create."

"Right now, at this moment, I am able to create a deep sense of calm and serenity within me."

"I control stress—it does not control me."

* * *

Notice how different these passages are from the kind of 'negative' self-talk we saw earlier. (*I can't do it; Nothing ever goes right for me; I can't handle this!; I'm stressed out; I'm at my wits end; I never get a break . . .*) The new, better kind of self-talk is not only positive, it is designed to give clear, new directions to your brain.

Is the New Self-Talk True of You?

When you first begin listening to self-talk, or practicing using self-talk phrases like those above, they may sound a little strange to you—especially if a lot of your old self-talk has been the negative kind. Hearing the new self-talk, you might think, *"That's not me,"* or *"That's not true about me."* But that's just your old, disbelieving mental programs trying to maintain their ground. Give the new self-talk time to do its work. In time, as they begin to be wired in as new 'truths' in your brain, the new messages will also become true about you.

Remember, the new self-talk is setting the record straight. It is replacing the old, negative, faulty programs with the kind of positive *'I can do it'* programs you should have received in the first place.

More Examples of Self-Talk for Stress

Here are some additional examples of the kinds of self-talk that will help you reduce stress. But this time, instead of dealing only with the stress itself, the examples focus on what is *causing* the stress.

The kind of self-talk I recommend for countering stress includes areas such as health, relationships, your job, and your finances, along with other areas that are often the *causes* of stress.

"I am strong, capable, and willing to do what I need to do to make my life work."

"I am healthy and fit. I take good care of myself, and it shows."

"I choose to be a healthy person. I see myself as active, energetic, and fit. That's the kind of person I choose to be."

"I have faith. My spirit, my belief, and my personal strength are alive and well within me."

"I have a good attitude about money and income. When it comes to having financial security in my life, I choose it, and I create it."

"I'm good at dealing with problems in a positive way."

"I get along with others, in every area of my life."

"I am a person who has positive relationships. That means that I create relationships that work."

"No matter what the problem or challenge may be, I am determined to deal with it, overcome it, get past it, and do better because of it."

"I have meaning and purpose in my life."

"By having a purpose in my life, I create more value in everything I do."

"Today I choose to take control of my life, decide what I want to do next, set my goals, and put myself into action."

"I'm on top, in tune, in touch, and going for it!"

* * *

As you read those passages, it is again easy to see the difference between the old kind of negative self-talk we have allowed to wire our brains for stress, and the very different kind of self-talk we see here.

The right self-talk wires your brain to focus on finding solutions, taking action, creating more self-confidence, and giving you more peace of mind—exactly the mental states that help you get rid of stress.

Self-Talk and 'Affirmations'

The terms 'self-talk' and 'affirmations' are often used incorrectly as synonyms for one another, but they're not the same.

Affirmations do "affirm." But in today's context, affirmations are statements that are most often used in spiritually or holistically oriented forms of self-expression, such as, *"I am at peace, and one with the divine universe."* That can be a good affirmation, but the self-talk used to direct your own programming each day, when you take control of your brain's neuroplastic imprinting, has to be more specific than that.

When you want to change neural pathways in your brain, your self-talk has to be precise, direct, and to the point: *"I get things done. I take action. I set clear, specific goals. I work at them, and I reach them."* Or, *"When I want to relax, I take three deep breaths, hold each of them for a moment, and release them."* Those kinds of targeted directions tell your brain exactly what to do and how to do it. In your brain, they create specific, directed results.

The self-talk that says, *"I get up at 6:15 each morning,"* is not an affirmation in the spiritual sense. It is a specific direction to your brain, telling it exactly what you choose to do. With the self-talk we're discussing here, you are like the pilot of an airplane programming precise directions into the airplane's onboard computer. (Flight officers never type *affirmations* into the airplane's navigational system; they type *directions*.)

Affirmations tend to create a softer, more general spiritual environment of the mind. If you've been using and practicing affirmations in the past, it doesn't hurt to keep using them. But when your goal is to wire your brain with a new language and new directions, use clear, specific and detailed self-talk, so your brain learns the language and knows *exactly* what to do next.

Why We Use Self-Talk in the 'Present Tense'

When you read or listen to any well-constructed self-talk, you'll find it is written in the present tense. For example, let's say you set a goal to spend 30 minutes a day improving yourself.

If you were to use self-talk that says, *"I'm going to spend 30 minutes a day improving myself,"* what message would that actually give to your brain? It would say, "I'm *'going'* to . . ." Which says, *"later,"* or *"some other time,"* or *"when I get around to it."*

If, as another example, you want to lose weight, instead of saying, *"I'm going to lose 15 pounds,"* give your brain a completed picture of what you want to accomplish: *"I choose to weigh 110 slim, trim, healthy, attractive pounds."* That's the picture your brain will see, and that's the slim, trim, healthy, attractive you your brain will help you create. You're saying, *"This is the me I choose to be. This is the me I want you to create. Here's the exact picture of what I want you to do."*

Always give your brain the most complete picture you can give it. That's the picture your brain will help you bring to life.

* * *

We've looked at examples of negative self-talk, how self-talk works in the brain and why it's important. We've also seen examples of the kind of positive self-talk that will get you thinking in the right direction, and program your mind to help you reduce stress and anxiety. Now let's look at how to put what we've learned into practice.

Chapter Eight

Changing Your Self-Talk

I have always felt that the most important part of my work with the Self-Talk Institute is in helping people apply what we've learned about self-talk—helping them actually put it into practice. Knowing how programming works in the brain is important, but practicing self-talk in everyday life is what counts.

To help people do that, the Institute offers a helpful *"Guide to Changing Your Self-Talk."* The guide is based on the Institute's thirty-five years of work in this area, and it identifies four key steps that anyone can follow. (You can download the Institute's guide at no cost at www.selftalkplus.com/guide.)

These are the four steps I would recommend to you if I were coaching you personally. I have summarized them for you here:

Step 1. Monitor

Monitor means to actively listen to your *current* self-talk. To get into the habit of doing this, practice monitoring everything you *say*, and everything you *think,* for a minimum of the next 30 days.

That's something anyone can do, but it takes some effort. Most of us aren't in the habit of examining every thought we have, or consciously reflecting on everything we say. But, when you practice paying attention to everything you think or say for an entire month, you learn *exactly* what self-talk—good or bad—is in control in your life right now.

Imagine that you asked someone to record *everything* you said for the next 30 days. Then, at the end of the 30 days, you printed out a transcript of everything you had said, so you could read it. Let's also imagine that, using a yellow marker, you highlighted every word or phrase in the transcript that was *repeated*. When you read those highlighted words and phrases, you would have a clear picture of what your self-talk is today. That transcript, of course, would not include the thousands of thoughts you *think* each day—and those thoughts are just as powerful as the things you say out loud!

If you could read a transcript of everything you said for the last 30 days, what would your daily 'mind script' look like? What kinds of things are you saying and thinking each day? Are they positive and uplifting? Do they let you know what you *can* do instead of what you can't? Do they describe you living up to your best—or do they show you a picture of you that is less than you'd like it to be?

Instead of having someone record your self-talk and print it out for you, making the decision to start listening to *everything* you say or think for the next few weeks will accomplish the same goal. It will tell you what your self-talk is right now, and it will give you important clues about the self-talk you're using that is contributing to your stress and anxiety—or even *causing* it.

Step 2. Edit

Everyone, with a little effort, has the ability to stop anything negative they are about to think or say, turn it around, and think or say the opposite—something that helps them instead of hurts them.

Edit means to change anything you were about to think or say—that could be harmful—and replace it with self-talk that is immediately positive and helpful. *Anything* you would have said that is negative, harmful, or could work against you should be replaced with new, on-the-spot positive self-talk that will help you.

When you're learning to edit your self-talk, you're taking a first step in taking responsibility for your own mental programming. But, just as with learning to monitor, you have to practice editing in order to create an automatic *habit* of doing it. Most of us aren't used to editing our words and thoughts to be more positive, so this may take some practice.

If you want to get good at changing your self-talk and reducing your stress, editing your words is *essential*. Editing, by itself, won't get rid of the old, negative programs you already have stored in your brain—but it will stop you from getting any more of the same.

Step 3. Listen

To learn the new language of positive self-talk in the shortest possible time, the Self-Talk Institute recommends listening to recorded sessions of self-talk. Listening to self-talk in this way uses the same method that's used to learn any new language—by repeated listening to it.

This step is optional, but it can greatly speed up the reprogramming process.

Listening to self-talk works well because it replaces and erases the old negative programs your brain has stored. As you listen, the repetition wires the new programs into your brain, and your brain begins to delete the negative programs you are no longer using. You will, by listening, be learning a 'new language.'

Also, because the new self-talk is positive, it is very motivating and uplifting to listen to— especially in the morning. It's a healthy way to start your day. (To listen to self-talk audio sessions, go to www.selftalkplus.com.)

Step 4. Practice

Practice means actively looking for the opportunities, the times each day when you have a chance to change your self-talk— including your thoughts—to create a different frame of mind. Most days will give many of those opportunities.

This is especially helpful when you're working at lowering your stress. Every time you feel stress coming on, and you first notice the negative or worried thoughts it brings with it, immediately turn those thoughts around— *change* them. Replace every troubling thought with self-talk that is healthy, strong, and confident. Practice this until it becomes a new habit, and a new kind of 'positive mindfulness' steps in and takes over, anytime stress is triggered.

An important note: Actively practicing getting rid of old thought patterns and replacing them with the right self-talk, doesn't mean you're suddenly trying to see the world through rose-colored glasses, painting a false picture of optimism, and ignoring the realities of your life.

Practicing the right self-talk encourages you to see the world as it is—no matter how difficult—and deal with it. But it does so in a way that also keeps you mindful of your strengths and the positive possibilities that are available to you. No one is more at risk of giving in to despair than the person who loses hope, and can no longer believe. And no one is stronger than the person who sees the light of possibility in front of them, and takes each step forward with courage and conviction.

* * *

If you want to change your self-talk, those are the steps to take. I have watched those simple steps work for countless people over many years. By learning to change their self-talk, people who thought they would never be free of endless stress and crippling anxiety have woken up to a life that was brighter and happy again.

If you want to have less stress and anxiety in your life, I encourage you to follow those steps.

Anyone can follow them, they work, and they will be well worth the effort.

Chapter Nine

Breaking the Cycle of Stress

In Chapter One of this book, I said that the cycle of negative self-talk and stress, anxiety, and depression can be broken. And as we have learned, it *can* be.

I'd like to encourage you. Even though it may have taken a long time for life to have generated the negative programs you accumulated along the way, it doesn't take another lifetime to get rid of them. In just weeks of time instead of years, you can experience the beginning of the reemergence of the real you—the wonderful, promising person you were born to be in the first place.

Imagine for a moment that there were two of you. One of you learned about self-talk and how to change it, and immediately began monitoring, editing, listening and practicing. Let's say this 'you' stayed with it, and was determined to get better, and get free—no more debilitating stress, no more endless anxiety, no more days of dark depression.

Meanwhile, let's say the *other* you did not learn about self-talk or did not figure it out, and did not make the choice to get rid of negative self-talk forever.

In a few months, or in a year from now, which one of the two you's would you vote for? Which one of you has the greatest chance of overcoming the negatives and the stress for good?

It would be the you who changed your self-talk, of course.

Your self-talk—right now—is both repeating the programs your brain has been wired with in the past, and it is also wiring new programs into your brain in this moment. That means your self-talk, right now, is wiring your brain—correctly or incorrectly—*and it will continue to do that every day of your life.*

Knowing that, it makes sense to get your wiring right. We may not be responsible for not taking control over our self-talk when we didn't know how much it mattered. But knowing what we now understand about self-talk and how the brain gets wired by our words and thoughts, it is both a responsibility and a blessing to be able to do something about it.

What is especially exciting to me about this process—changing your wiring so your life works better—is that when you do it, it works; you can start feeling the difference almost immediately. I get to meet or hear from so many people who have done exactly that. Their lives have changed in so many positive ways. I wish *you* could meet all of them!

Their stories are the stories of lives that are working! So many people who once lived in fear, dreading the next day, literally suffocating from anxiety, have found new freedom and new hope, because they learned about self-talk, and about rewiring their brain, and they decided to do it.

No matter where you are in your life today, I hope you will do what they did. Decide to get rid of every last negative mental program that is weighing you down or holding you back. Let the old programs go. They're not helping you, and you don't need them any longer.

You have so much to live for. There is a reason you are here, a purpose for your being. And like that infant in the newborn nursery who was born with unlimited potential and endless positive possibilities, that great promise you were born with never went away. It lives within you still!

Imagine bringing that promise to light, moving past the pain, past the stress, past the anxiety and the depression, into a new sunlight, a new future. Imagine what you can do!

That is the promise that is yours. And with the right self-talk, the healthy words of living helping to make things right, and bringing you back into the light, you will see it too.

Shad Helmstetter, Ph.D.
August, 2020

Tools and Resources

To Listen to Self-Talk:
www.selftalkplus.com

To Become a Certified Self-Talk Trainer:
www.selftalkinstitute.com

For Life Coach Training:
www.lifecoachinstitute.com

For a Free Life Coach Session
with an LCI Certified Life Coach:
www.selftalkplus.com/personal-life-
coaching-session/

To Contact Dr. Helmstetter:
Email shadhelmstetteroffice@gmail.com

Made in the USA
Las Vegas, NV
22 November 2022